I0798664

STUDY GUIDE

Reformation Profiles

Stephen J. Nichols

LIGONIER MINISTRIES
Renew your Mind.
LIGONIER.ORG | 800-435-4343

Copyright © 2012 Ligonier Ministries
421 Ligonier Court, Sanford, FL 32771
E-mail: info@ligonier.org
All rights reserved.
No reproduction of this work without permission.
Printed in the United States of America.

1

Why the Reformation Matters

MESSAGE INTRODUCTION

The author of Ecclesiastes states, "What has been is what will be, and what has been done is what will be done, and there is nothing new under the sun" (Eccl. 1:9). Apart from the theological significance of this profound statement, another observation arises concerning the study of history: it matters. Although time progresses in a linear direction and contains unique, monumental events (culminating in the return of Jesus), creation witnesses the repetition of patterns, movements, and interactions between humans. The church today faces problems similar to the church of yesteryear, albeit packaged and branded in different forms. A careful study of the history of the church prepares and equips its members to face the difficulties of its own day. The Reformation of the sixteenth century emphasized a return to the Word of God as a remedy for the theological deficiencies of the Roman Catholic Church, and Dr. Nichols embarks on this series to assist the current church by understanding the *solas* of the Reformation and their place for the people of God in all ages.

SCRIPTURE READINGS

Genesis 22; Psalm 68:19–20; 136; John 3:16

TEACHING OBJECTIVES

1. To illuminate the context physically and spiritually from which the Reformation emerged
2. To demonstrate the importance of studying the Reformation
3. To present an introduction to the *solas* and an outline of the progression of this teaching series

QUOTATION

In the very midst of life, snares of death surround us. Who shall help us in this strife, lest the foe confound us? Thou only, Lord, Thou only. In the midst of death's dark veil, powers of hell overtake us. Who will help when they assail? Who secure will make us? Thou only, Lord, Thou only. In the midst of utter woe, when our sins oppress us, where shall we for refuge go? Where for grace to bless us? To Thee, Lord Jesus, only. Thy precious blood was shed to win, full atonement for our sin.

—from Martin Luther's hymn, "In the Very Midst of Life"

LECTURE OUTLINE

I. From Death to Life, From Darkness to Light
  - A. The harsh, plague-ridden conditions in Europe during the Middle Ages (circa AD 500 to 1500), also called the "Dark Ages," forced Europeans to face and accept mortality and death.
    - i. Death surrounded the people, and they did not possess the faculty and knowledge to challenge it, so they accepted it.
    - ii. The common saying *Media vita in morte sumus*, meaning, "In the midst of life, we die," originated and circulated in the medieval times.
  - B. The darkness percolating spiritually during the Middle Ages resembled the bleak physical conditions of the times.
  - C. The Reformation occurred in this era, and out of death and darkness came life and light through the power of the gospel of Jesus Christ.
    - i. Martin Luther turned the phrase, "In the midst of life, we die," on its head by pointing to the gospel and stating, "In the midst of death, we live."
    - ii. To demonstrate the emergence from spiritual darkness, the city of Geneva, under the leadership of John Calvin, took up the motto *Post tenebras lux*, meaning "After darkness, light."

II. Why We Study the Reformation
  - A. History matters
    - i. Christians possess a historic faith, at the center of which resides a historical Savior.
    - ii. God calls His people to look back at His redemptive work on their behalf to remind them of their relationship.
      1. The Bible continually commands this exercise, from the earliest of God's people to ancient Israel to new covenant believers.
      2. The Holy Spirit works in God's people at every stage of history, and, therefore, each stage of church history remains important for all believers at all times.
  - B. The Reformation captured, or recaptured, the essence of the church's purpose.

i. By the time of the Reformation, everyone, the church included, recognized the detestable state of the church.
    1. The period between the thirteenth and sixteenth century, referred to as the later medieval age or the High Middles Ages, witnessed significant deterioration in the Roman Catholic Church.
    2. Many attempted to reform the church.
        a. The Conciliar Movement attempted an administrative reform in the Roman Catholic Church by calling for a shift of power to the more ancient form of in the church, a council of bishops.
            1) The famous Czech reformer, John Hus, belonged to this movement.
            2) The movement did not succeed.
        b. Many advocated a spiritual reform in the church, called the *Devotio Moderna*, the "new devotion."
            1) Thomas À Kempis, the author of *The Imitation of Christ*, belonged to this movement.
            2) While marginally successful, the movement did not succeed.
    3. The reform movements, while commendable, failed to diagnose the true problem: theological rottenness.

ii. The Reformers of the sixteenth century recognized the theological deficiency extant in the Roman Catholic Church and they prescribed the proper solution: return to the centrality of the Word of God.
    1. A theological shortcoming needed a theological solution.
    2. The Reformers infused proper theology into preaching, Christian education, missions, and more.

C. The church faces similar challenges today, and we can learn particular things from them to assist us.
    i. This teaching series will set out to accomplish this task by examining the *solas* of the Reformation in conjunction with biographical sketches.
    ii. We will learn the purpose and nature of the *solas*, how they connect to Scripture, and how they connect to being a disciple of Christ.

D. The Reformers, real people with real lives, give us insight into what it means to be a Christian.

III. The Five *Solas*

A. *Sola Scriptura*: "Scripture alone"
    i. The issue concerns authority.
        1. Tradition has a valuable place in the church.
        2. However, tradition always submits to Scripture, a principle the Reformers felt the Roman Catholic Church had abandoned.
    ii. We will examine the life of Martin Luther in conjunction with *sola Scriptura*.

B. *Sola gratia*: "Grace alone"; *Sola fide*: "Faith alone"

   i. The gospel comes through grace alone and is received by faith alone.
   ii. We will examine the life of Ulrich Zwingli in conjunction with *sola gratia*.
   iii. We will examine the life of Lady Jane Grey in conjunction with *sola fide*.

C. *Solus Christus*: "Christ alone"
   i. Salvation comes only through Christ, the lone Mediator between God and man.
   ii. We will examine the life of John Calvin in conjunction with *solus Christus*.

D. *Soli Deo Gloria*: "The glory of God alone"
   i. All of creation and redemption serve the glory of God alone.
   ii. We will examine the lives of the Puritans in conjunction with *soli Deo gloria*.

STUDY QUESTIONS

1. The Middle Ages are also called the "Dark Ages" because death and spiritual darkness surrounded the people living within this period of history.
   a. True
   b. False

2. *Post tenebras lux* means ____________.
   a. "With darkness comes light"
   b. "Darkness and light mingled"
   c. "After darkness, light"
   d. "Light breaks into the darkness"

3. The Conciliar Movement succeeded in reforming the administration of the Roman Catholic Church.
   a. True
   b. False

4. What was the primary solution the Reformers posited to cure the theological deficiency of the Roman Catholic Church?
   a. Replace the Pope
   b. Move the seat of central authority from Rome
   c. Return to the Word of God
   d. Emphasize tradition more

5. The study of history, particularly the Reformation, matters today because the church faces similar problems in our era.
   a. True
   b. False

BIBLE STUDY AND DISCUSSION QUESTIONS

1. Why do historians refer to the Middle Ages as the "Dark Ages"? How did the Reformation challenge and confront the problems contributing to the darkness of this period of history?

2. Why does history matter, particularly for the church?

3. How did the Reformation capture the essence of the church's purpose? What reformation movements did Dr. Nichols describe that occurred prior to the Reformation of the sixteenth century? Did these movements succeed? Why or why not? What did the Reformers view as the primary deficiency within the Roman Catholic Church, and what remedy did they present?

4. Does the church face similar problems today as the Reformers faced in the sixteenth century? If so, what are some of these problems? How does the study of history assist the church in facing these difficulties and obstacles?

5. List and define the five *solas*.

2

Sola Scriptura: Martin Luther & the Rediscovery of the Authority of Scripture

MESSAGE INTRODUCTION

In the early sixteenth century, illiteracy was the norm across Europe, and this condition existed even amongst the clergy, teachers of God's Word. Yet, despite the enormity of this problem, a deeper dilemma remained: the place of the Word of God had shifted in the Roman Catholic Church. No longer did the Bible stand as the central authority upon which the Christian life rested. Tradition, much of it corrupt and driven by the financial bankruptcy of the papal seat in Rome, had displaced it. God, in His gracious providence, did not allow this condition to persist. He raised up a humble monk from Germany, Martin Luther, to take a stand against the church on the principle of *sola Scriptura* ("Scripture alone"). This stand sparked the flame of the Reformation that burned through Europe and continues to blaze throughout the world today.

SCRIPTURE READINGS

Matthew 24:32–36; Romans 1:16–18; 1 Peter 1:22–25

TEACHING OBJECTIVES

1. To describe the life of Martin Luther
2. To explain the experiences and studies leading to Luther's authorship of the ninety-five theses
3. To illustrate how Luther's dedication to the principle of *sola Scriptura* led him to take a stand before the Roman Catholic Church and to the Protestant Reformation of the sixteenth century

QUOTATION

> *Since your Majesty and your Lordships ask for a plain answer, I will give you one without either horns or teeth. Unless I am convicted by Scripture or by right reason (for I trust neither in popes nor in councils, since they have often erred and contradicted themselves)—unless I am thus convinced, I am bound by the texts of the Bible, my conscience is captive to the Word of God.*
>
> —Martin Luther at the Diet of Worms, taken from R.C. Sproul's book *Faith Alone*

LECTURE OUTLINE

I. The Life of Martin Luther
   A. Youth and development (AD 1483–1505)
      i. Luther was born into a hardworking, German family.
         1. Luther was born on November 10, 1483, to Hans and Margarethe Luther.
         2. Hans, an ambitious man, worked in and supervised the mines in order to provide Martin with a chance to attend university and study law.
      ii. As a result of his parents sacrifice, Luther enrolled in the university at Erfurt.
         1. After completing a bachelor's and a master's degree, Luther returned home from law school to visit his family.
            a. During this trip, a thunderstorm struck while Luther was out in the open, and he took cover under a tree on the top of a hill.
            b. The ferocity of the storm drove Luther to believe God was unleashing His wrath and anger on him, and Luther clung to a rock under the tree in fear.
            c. In a moment of terror, Luther cried out to Saint Anne, the patron saint of miners (the profession of his father), saying, "Help me, Saint Anne, and I will become a monk."
         2. Luther survived the storm, returned to Erfurt, left law school, and entered a monastery.
   B. The soul-struggles (German: *anfechtungen*) of Luther (AD 1505–1517)
      i. Luther entered an Augustinian monastery in 1505.
         1. Luther began as a novice, a position held for two years.
            a. During this time, Luther would spend five hours performing the sacrament of confession.
            b. Needless to say, this greatly perturbed the confessors.
         2. After two years, Luther was ordained as a priest and attempted to deliver his first mass.
            a. Traditionally, at a certain point in the mass, the priest officiating the mass would say, "To Thee, the living, eternal God."
               1) Due to fear, Luther could not bring himself to utter these words.
               2) This failure embarrassed Luther, his family, and the monastery.

b. Following this incident, the monastery sent Luther to seminary to study theology.

ii. During his time at seminary, Luther read Peter Lombard's *The Sentences*.

1. To qualify for a doctor of theology, students had to memorize, debate, and defend *The Sentences*.
2. In his writing, Lombard quoted Augustine of Hippo frequently.
   a. Through Augustine, Luther learned that the problem humans have is not the quantity of sins they commit.
   b. The problem is that humans are sinners at the root (Latin: *radix*).
   c. Luther realized that no amount of penance or indulgence could overcome this condition.

iii. After completing his studies, Luther's monastery sent him to the Pope at Rome as an emissary.

1. The monastery needed the Pope to renew its credentials.
2. While in Rome, Luther became disillusioned over the extortion of pilgrims by the Roman Catholic Church, even uttering the phrase, "Who knows if all of this is true" while climbing the *Scala Sancta* ("Holy Stairs": presumably the stairs Jesus climbed to reach Pilate in Jerusalem).

iv. When Luther returned to Germany, his monastery sent him to Wittenberg to teach at the university there.

1. Frederick the Wise, the founder of the university of Wittenberg, wanted to compete with the greatest intellectual centers of the day, and the seminary recommended Luther for a position of theology.
2. The university assigned Luther to teach the books of Psalms, Romans, Galatians, and Hebrews.
   a. Luther's study of these books from 1513–1517, in conjunction with his visit to Rome, led him to believe that something was amiss in the Roman Catholic Church.
   b. Luther developed ninety-five theses as a counter-proposal to the activity of Rome, particularly the selling of indulgences.
   c. Luther understood that sin does not involve a scale of demerit and merit to which man perpetually contributes.
   d. Through his study of God's Word and his own experiences, Luther realized that man's sinful nature needs a transformation that can only come from outside of himself. This transformation occurs through the atonement and righteousness of Jesus Christ, which His Spirit applies to passive believers.
3. Upon hearing of the ninety-five theses, the Pope dismissed it as vain, effervescent rambling from which Luther would soon sober. He did not.

C. The fallout from the ninety-five theses (AD 1517–1546)

i. Luther proceeded to write three treatises against the Roman Catholic Church.

1. He titled one of these treatises, *Prelude on the Babylonian Captivity of the Church.*
2. The treatise attacked the Roman Catholic understanding of their seven sacraments in light of Biblical evidence.

ii. The Pope responded by issuing a papal decree against Luther.

1. The decree claimed Luther was a wild boar trampling in the vineyard of Christ and appealed to the Lord to "rise up" (Latin: *Exsurge Domine*).
2. Luther burned the papal bull.

iii. Luther was called to defend himself at the Diet of Worms, where he defended the principle of *sola Scriptura* ("Scripture alone") and stated that Popes have erred and contradicted one another and that his conscience was captive to the Word of God.

iv. Following the Diet of Worms, Luther went into hiding and exile at Wartburg Castle.

v. Luther eventually returned to Wittenberg and established a church.

1. Luther engaged in a dynamic, prolific ministry for the rest of his life.
2. At the center of everything Luther did stood the centrality of the Word of God.

STUDY QUESTIONS

1. In a moment of terror during a severe thunderstorm, Luther guaranteed his entrance into the monastery if Saint Michael would intervene and save him.
   a. True
   b. False

2. Luther did not take confession seriously during his time as a novice, much to the dismay of his confessors.
   a. True
   b. False

3. While studying for his doctor of theology, Luther read *The Sentences*, written by ____________.
   a. Augustine of Hippo
   b. John Calvin
   c. Thomas Aquinas
   d. Peter Lombard

4. Luther's time in Rome confirmed to him that the problem in the Roman Catholic Church existed only in Germany.
   a. True
   b. False

5. Where was Luther called to testify concerning his position on Rome and his ninety-five theses?
   a. The Council of Trent
   b. The Diet of Worms
   c. The Council if Chalcedon
   d. The Synod of Marseille

BIBLE STUDY AND DISCUSSION QUESTIONS

1. Describe Luther's episode with the thunderstorm during his time away from university. How did Luther respond to the storm? How was Luther's response indicative of general understanding of mediation in the Roman Catholic Church?

2. What did Luther learn from reading *The Sentences*? Where in Scripture would you look to support this understanding?

3. What did Luther discover at Rome? Why did it disillusion him?

4. What led to Martin Luther writing the ninety-five theses? What is an indulgence? Why did Luther choose this point at the center of his attack?

5. How did Luther come to believe in the doctrine of *sola Scriptura*? How did this defy the beliefs of his day? Does Scripture support this view? Provide evidence from Scripture.

3

Sola Gratia: Ulrich Zwingli & the Rediscovery of Grace

MESSAGE INTRODUCTION

Most religious convictions in popular culture boil down to some activity or practice on the part of the individual to better their circumstances or perspective on life. Regardless of the manifestation of the principle, it all simmers down to this fact: mankind continually looks internally for solutions that he can only find externally. In the sixteenth century, the Roman Catholic Church rested under this misapprehension. It had created a system of merit integral for salvation and incumbent upon works. The weight of these demands crushed Christians throughout Europe. Hence, as Ulrich Zwingli read and preached the Word of God in the city of Zurich, it is no wonder he delighted at the principle of *sola gratia* ("grace alone") and Jesus' declaration that His "yoke is easy and [His] burden is light." Zwingli realized that the grace of God in Jesus released His followers from an unbearable burden of righteousness.

SCRIPTURE READINGS

Matthew 11:25–30; 1 Corinthians 8:1–13; 11:17–34

TEACHING OBJECTIVES

1. To understand how the providential life experiences of Zwingli contributed to his impact on the Reformation and the city of Zurich
2. To illuminate some of the views on the Lord's Supper during the Reformation
3. To demonstrate how Zwingli's understanding of the Word of God freed him of the legalistic burdens of the Roman Catholic Church and allowed him to champion the principle of *sola gratia* ("grace alone").

QUOTATION

Through Christ alone we are given salvation, blessedness, grace, pardon, and all that makes us in any way worthy in the sight of a righteous God.

—Ulrich Zwingli, from his *Commentary on True and False Religion*

LECTURE OUTLINE

I. The Life of Ulrich Zwingli (AD 1484–1531)
  A. The pre-sausage-supper period (prior to AD 1519)
    i. Zwingli studied at the University of Vienna and the University of Basel.
      1. During his time at Basel (AD 514–516), Zwingli interacted with Erasmus, the scholar responsible for compiling and printing a Greek text of the New Testament.
      2. Zwingli probably assisted Erasmus in this project.
    ii. After graduating from Basel, Zwingli received a pastoral charge at a location with a Marian apparition on the side of a cliff.
      1. In the morning, Zwingli would give the mass to pilgrims.
      2. Zwingli would retreat to his home after the mass and study, and he devoted particular attention to Erasmus' Greek text of the New Testament.
    iii. In 1518, Zwingli learned of an opening for the position of the people's priest at the Grossmünster ("Great Minster") in the city of Zurich.
      1. Zwingli applied for the job and was appointed to the position.
      2. On January 1, 1519, Zwingli began to preach at the Grossmünster, and he began in Matthew 1:1 with the intent to preach through the entire New Testament.
  B. The sausage-supper period (AD 1519–1523)
    i. While preaching through the New Testament at the Grossmünster, Zwingli began to discover that much of what he had learned under the tutelage of the church did not exist in Scripture.
    ii. In 1521, Zwingli held a supper during Lent (the period of six weeks leading up to Easter) at which he cooked and served sausage.
      1. Roman Catholicism traditionally forbade the eating of meat on Fridays during Lent.
      2. Many of the leaders of city participated in this supper and ate the sausage Zwingli prepared. (Zwingli abstained from eating it.)
    iii. The following Sunday, Zwingli preached a sermon titled "On the Choice and Freedom of Foods."
      1. Zwingli stated in the sermon that he did not find justification for Lent in Scripture.
      2. Zwingli had come to realize that layers of tradition had obscured the truth of the Word of God.

- iv. That same year, Zwingli published a tract titled, "On the Ability for Priests to Marry."
  1. The tract advocated marriage amongst the clergy.
  2. This tract also demonstrated that Zwingli and many of his congregants believed that the church had added improper rules and regulations to Scripture.
- v. In 1522, the city of Zurich held two disputations to determine the stand of the city on reformation.
  1. During the disputations, Zwingli argued from Scripture against Roman Catholicism and advocated for Zurich to become a Reformed city.
  2. Zwingli and his supporters won, and Zurich became the first Reformed city in Switzerland.
  3. Many Swiss cities followed Zurich's example.

C. The post-sausage-supper period

- i. Following this declaration, Zwingli entered a radical phase in his ministry and began to dismantle many items he believed outside of the advocacy of Scripture.
- ii. The Anabaptists began in Zurich under Conrad Grebel (an attendee of the sausage supper) in the wake of Zurich's secession.
  1. This Radical Reformation/Anabaptist movement wanted to break from the state entirely.
  2. In contrast to the Reformers, the Anabaptists adhered to believer's baptism, re-baptizing each other because they believed infant baptism, particularly under the Roman Catholic Church, unbiblical.
  3. Zwingli would experience much confrontation with this movement.
- iii. Martin Luther and Zwingli began corresponding in this period, and they entered into a dispute over the Lord's Supper during their correspondence.
  1. The Roman Catholic Church held to a view of the Lord's Supper called transubstantiation (which it still holds today). This view stated that the bread and the wine of the Lord's Supper transformed into the substance of Christ upon the priest's pronouncement.
  2. Luther rejected this view and developed a view of the Lord's Supper called consubstantiation ("with substance"). (Luther did not like this term.) This view held that the real presence of Christ is all around the elements of the Lord's Supper.
  3. Zwingli rejected this view in favor of his view, the memorial view. This view stated that the elements of the Lord's Supper served merely as signs pointing to the death of Jesus.
  4. With the Roman Catholic Church pressuring the Lutheran and Reformed churches of Germany and Switzerland from the West, and Islam pressing in from the East, the leaders of these Protestant churches called a colloquy to resolve these differences and to form a united front.

iv. Luther and Zwingli, along with the leaders of the Lutheran and Reformed churches, assembled at the Marburg Colloquy in 1529.
    1. Luther and Zwingli agreed on all points of doctrine except the Lord's Supper.
    2. Although both presented their arguments, they could not agree and the churches remained separated.
    3. Years later, John Calvin offered his view of the Lord's Supper, the spiritual view. This view stated that Christ is present spiritually at the Lord's Supper, and Luther admitted that had Calvin presented this view at Marburg, he and Zwingli may have agreed on this middle road.

v. Zwingli established a school for pastors in Zurich called "The Prophetzei."
    1. Classes began with the book of Genesis and worked consecutively until the end of the Bible.
    2. In the Old Testament, lecturers read from the Hebrew and Greek texts and commented on them. (They read only the Greek when they entered the New Testament.)
    3. Following the lectures from the original languages, a scholar would teach in Latin on the theology and tradition of the text.
    4. Finally, a parish priest would finish the day by preaching from the selected text of the day in German.
    5. This school would eventually become the University of Zurich, and the curriculum demonstrated Zwingli's passion for the authority and importance of the Word of God.

vi. Zwingli died in 1531 in battle at Kappel while serving as a chaplain.
    1. Zwingli's true legacy remains his adherence to the principle of *sola gratia* ("grace alone").
    2. Zwingli realized that the Roman Catholic Church had heaped burden upon burden on the people, and it had called them to engage in works to remove these weights.
    3. From reading God's Word, Zwingli understood that Jesus' "yoke is easy, and [His] burden is light" (Matt. 11:30). God is not a legalistic God, but a God of grace desirous to give His people rest.

STUDY QUESTIONS

1. During his time at Basel, Zwingli worked on the Greek text of the New Testament with ____________.
    a. John Calvin
    b. Martin Luther
    c. Conrad Grebel
    d. Erasmus

2. In 1519, Zwingli took a position as the people's priest in Zurich at ___________.
   a. Grossmünster
   b. Fraumünster
   c. St. Peterskirche
   d. Westminster

3. Zwingli broke Roman Catholic tradition by preparing and serving meat during the Advent season.
   a. True
   b. False

4. Zwingli was exiled from Zurich because he advocated the city to declare itself reformed.
   a. True
   b. False

5. Luther and Zwingli disagreed severely on the nature of Christ's presence in the Lord's Supper.
   a. True
   b. False

BIBLE STUDY AND DISCUSSION QUESTIONS

1. What did Zwingli discover while preaching through the Bible at his post at the Grossmünster. How did he respond during Lent in 1521? Why was this infraction so horrendous, and what did it represent about Zwingli and his parishioners?

2. After the incident during Lent, what other steps did Zwingli take to demonstrate his position on Roman Catholic tradition? How did the city respond? After the decision of the city, what steps did Zwingli take and why?

3. Explain the nature of the conflict between Luther and Zwingli over the Lord's Supper? Who is right? Why? Present your arguments from Scripture. Did Calvin have the correct, biblical position?

4. Explain the process Zwingli instituted in his school in Zurich. Why did Zwingli create such a curriculum?

5. How does Zwingli's life and ministry exemplify *sola gratia*?

4

Sola Fide: Lady Jane Grey & the Rediscovery of Justification by Faith

MESSAGE INTRODUCTION

After witnessing the remarkable deliverance of Paul and Silas from his prison, the Philippian jailer cried out to Paul, "What must I do to be saved?" (Acts 16:30). They responded, "Believe in the Lord Jesus, and you will be saved, you and your household" (v.31). Their exhortation to the Philippian jailer demonstrates that salvation comes through grace by faith alone. The Word of God is replete with similar assertions, and these instances enabled Lady Jane Grey to confront death with confidence that the salvation of her soul rested in the hands of her Savior and not her own.

SCRIPTURE READINGS

Romans 3:21–31; Ephesians 2:8–10

TEACHING OBJECTIVES

1. To demonstrate how Lady Jane's belief in salvation by grace through faith alone (*sola gratia* and *sola fide*) fortified her to defend the truth of Scripture and face death
2. To explain the doctrine of justification as defined by the Reformers

QUOTATION

I have here sent you, good sister Catherine, a book, which although it be not outwardly trimmed with gold yet inwardly it is more than precious stones. It is the dear book, my sister, of the law of the Lord. Rejoice in Christ as I do. Follow the steps of your master Christ and take up your cross. Lay your sins on His back, and always embrace Him. And as touching my death, rejoice as I do, good sister, that I shall be delivered of this corruption and put on incorruption. For I am assured that I shall, having lost my mortal life, shall win an immortal life.

—A note inscribed by Lady Jane in her Bible for her sister before her death

LECTURE OUTLINE

I. The Life of Lady Jane Grey (AD 1536/1537–1554)
   A. The historical context for Lady Jane's rise and fall
      i. In the years immediately following the death of Henry VIII of England, a number of successors rose to the throne.
         1. Edward VI, Henry's son by Jane Seymour, ascended to the throne in 1547, but he died thereafter in 1553.
         2. In an attempt to avoid the succession of Mary, Henry's eldest daughter and a Roman Catholic, Edward's Protestant advisors (called the "Privy Council") installed Lady Jane Grey (Edward's first cousin once removed) as the Queen of England.
      ii. Nine days after her coronation, the Privy Council switched its allegiance to Mary.
         1. Lady Jane was denounced as an usurper.
         2. She was taken to the Tower of London as a prisoner.
         3. In an attempt to cure Lady Jane of her heresy, Mary ordered her chaplain and confessor, John Feckenham, to attempt to convince Lady Jane of her errors.
   B. The debate between Lady Jane and John Feckenham
      i. Feckenham began the discussion by asking Lady Jane about the number of sacraments.
         1. Lady Jane stated that there were two sacraments: baptism and the Lord's Supper.
         2. Feckenham corrected her with the traditional Roman Catholic understanding that there are seven sacraments.
         3. Lady Jane asked Feckenham to provide evidence from Scripture for this view. Feckenham switched the subject.
      ii. Feckenham moved the topic from sacraments to justification.
         1. He scolded Lady Jane for taking her position on justification from the Reformers (e.g. Martin Luther) rather than from the church.
         2. Lady Jane responded that she came to her understanding of justification from Scripture, from which the Roman Catholic Church had deviated.
         3. This answer demonstrated Lady Jane's commitment to the principle of *sola Scriptura*.
      iii. In response to Lady Jane's answer, Feckenham proceeded to ask what God requires of Christians for their justification.
         1. Lady Jane stated that God required faith in the Trinity, from which Christians follow the two great commandments as summarized by Jesus.

2. Feckenham countered by turning to Paul's assertion that faith without love is nothing.
3. Lady Jane replied that they must go hand in hand.
4. Thinking that he had trapped her, Feckenham responded that acts of love must contribute to salvation.
5. Lady Jane denied this assertion and stated that works do not profit a person unto salvation but flow out of faith in the blood of Christ.

iv. Lady Jane was unable to be persuaded to recant her beliefs, and she was sentenced to death.
  1. Before her death, Lady Jane wrote a note in her Bible for her sister.
  2. The note called her sister to "rejoice in Christ" on account of His saving grace.
  3. Similar to Martin Luther, Lady Jane understood that the problem of sin is not its quantity in the life of a believer, but its presence in the heart.
     a. Luther, therefore, claimed that sinners need an "alien righteousness" outside of themselves to be reconciled before God.
     b. Lady Jane could rejoice in Christ on her deathbed because she held to *sola fide* ("faith alone"), and she believed that salvation came through grace by faith in the death and resurrection of her Lord and Savior, Jesus.

II. Justification and the Reformation
  A. As stated previously, Martin Luther developed the idea of "alien righteousness": a righteousness outside of the believer acquired by faith in Jesus.
  B. John Calvin categorized the causes of justification in his work, *The Institutes of the Christian Religion*.
    i. The efficient cause of justification is the free mercy and love of God.
    ii. The material cause of justification (what makes it happen) is the reconciling work of Jesus on the cross.
    iii. The instrumental cause of justification (what applies the material cause) is faith, produced by the regenerating work of the Holy Spirit.
    iv. The final cause is God's glory.
  C. The Reformers used the word *monergism* to describe this work of salvation.
    i. *Monergism* means "one work."
    ii. *Synergism* means "working together."
    iii. The Reformers understood the work of salvation to come from the power of God alone for His glory alone.
  D. Martin Luther used a second term to describe the doctrine of justification: *immediate*.
    i. This term means "without a mediator."
      1. God reconciles man to Himself through the work of Jesus.
      2. Over time, the Roman Catholic Church had inserted itself in a position of mediation between Jesus and man.

a. By inserting itself in this position, the church claimed that grace flowed through it.

b. One of the ways the church distributed grace to the people is by taking the grace received through the works of saints and other Christians beyond God's requirements and distributing it amongst other Christians. (The technical term is *supererogation*: "payment beyond what is due.")

ii. The Reformers employed the term *immediate* to demonstrate that the only mediator between God and man is Christ, and the grace that comes from Him can only be attained through faith engendered by the Holy Spirit.

STUDY QUESTIONS

1. Lady Jane reigned as queen over England for how long?
   a. Five hours
   b. Nine days
   c. Two months
   d. One year

2. Who did Mary send to convince Lady Jane to refute her beliefs.
   a. Thomas Wolsey
   b. Thomas Cranmer
   c. Richard Hooker
   d. John Feckenham

3. After inquisition and torture, Lady Jane recanted her beliefs and was restored to the royal court.
   a. True
   b. False

4. Monergism means "one work."
   a. True
   b. False

5. The Reformers believed the Roman Catholic Church had inappropriately inserted itself as a mediator between Jesus and men.
   a. True
   b. False

BIBLE STUDY AND DISCUSSION QUESTIONS

1. Describe the historical context leading to the ascension of Lady Jane to the throne of the English monarch. Why and how did she attain the crown? How and why did her reign end?

2. Describe the conversation between Lady Jane and John Feckenham. How did Lady Jane defend the doctrine of *sola fide*? How did her belief assist her during this time of her life?

3. List and explain John Calvin's categories for the causes of justification?

4. How did the Reformers understand the work of God in salvation? How did this differ from the Roman Catholic understanding of justification?

5. What does the term *alien righteousness* mean in connection with the doctrine of justification? Why did the Reformers use the term *immediate* in conjunction with the doctrine of justification? How did the Roman Catholic Church differ?

5

Solus Christus: John Calvin & the Blessing of Christ Alone

MESSAGE INTRODUCTION

Paul tells us in Romans 6:5 that "if we have been united with him in a death like his, we shall certainly be united with him in a resurrection like his." Paul writes these words to demonstrate the certainty of our union with Jesus in His resurrection and eternal life. In the United States and many other affluent countries, people avoid facing mortality, anesthetizing themselves in a multitude of ways. In the sixteenth century, this option generally did not exist, and John Calvin stood as no exception. He and his family struggled with illness and death throughout their lives, eventually succumbing to it earlier than expected. Nonetheless, Calvin clung to the promise of eternal life, letting it infuse and shape everything he did. He understood the principle of *solus Christus* ("Christ alone"), believing that the blessing of salvation by grace through faith alone awaits those who cling to our Lord and Savior, Jesus.

SCRIPTURE READINGS

Romans 5:10; 6:1–14; 8:12–17; Ephesians 1:3–14

TEACHING OBJECTIVES

1. To understand how Calvin's experiences providentially led and equipped him to serve the Lord faithfully as a pastor at Geneva
2. To demonstrate the role Geneva played in sending out missionaries and housing refugees
3. To illustrate how Calvin, one of the great Reformers of the church, used the doctrine of *solus Christus* ("Christ alone") to fuel his every endeavor and effort

QUOTATION

We must now examine this question. How do we receive those benefits which the Father bestowed on His only-begotten Son–not for Christ's own private use, but that He might enrich poor and needy men? First, we must understand that as long as Christ remains outside of us, and we are separated from Him, all that He has suffered and done for the salvation of the human race remains useless and of no value for us. Therefore, to share with us what He has received from the Father, He had to become ours and to dwell within us. For this reason, He is called 'our Head' (Eph. 4:15), and 'the first-born among many brethren' (Rom. 8:29). We also, in turn, are said to be 'engrafted into Him' (Rom. 11:17), and to 'put on Christ' (Gal. 3:27). For, as I have said, all that He possesses is nothing to us until we grow into one body with Him. It is true that we obtain this by faith.

—an excerpt from John Calvin's *Institutes of the Christian Religion*

LECTURE OUTLINE

I. The Life of John Calvin (AD 1509–1564)
   A. The early years
      i. Calvin was born in Noyon, France, on July 10, 1509.
      ii. At an early age, Calvin departed to study at the University of Paris to pursue a career in ministry.
         1. During his studies, Calvin became deeply involved in the humanities, and, consequently, he pushed aside his ministerial aspirations.
         2. Calvin entered the University of Bourges in 1529, and he wrote and published a commentary on Seneca the Younger's work *De Clementia*.
      iii. During this time, Calvin's roommate persuaded him to read some literature written by the Reformers, and he was converted in May of 1534.
   B. Post-conversion
      i. Within a year of his conversion, Calvin wrote a second book, a systematic theology.
         1. Calvin titled the book, *Institutes of the Christian Religion*.
            a. The first edition of the book was small, but Calvin continued to revise and add to it through the 1550s.
            b. Calvin published the book under the pseudonym, Martinus Lucianus.
               1) He honored Martin Luther with the first name.
               2) Calvin mixed up the letters of his last name for the surname of the pseudonym.
         2. The *Institutes* was circulated widely and well-received.
      ii. Calvin left France to study at Strasbourg under Martin Bucer.
         1. After experiencing pressure in France (a country that was divided over the Reformation), Calvin set out for Strasbourg in the North.
            a. Activity on the border of France forced Calvin to make a detour.
            b. Calvin detoured south through Geneva and met William Farel.

2. Farel desired for Calvin to stay in Geneva permanently.
    a. Farel, a minister in Geneva, had been beaten and exiled twice by the city before it accepted him as a minister.
    b. Despite a fiery and passionate nature for the Lord, Farel accepted his limitations and implored Calvin to stay in Geneva.
    c. Calvin wanted to stay only one night and did not desire to enter the ministry, but Farel stated that if Calvin did not stay and assist him in establishing the church in Geneva, God would curse him.
3. At the behest of Farel, Calvin remained in Geneva to assist in the establishment of the reformed church.

C. Calvin's first term in Geneva
- i. Calvin received resistance to his ministry on account of his French origin.
    1. The city referred to him as "that Frenchman."
    2. Swiss roots ran deep in Geneva.
- ii. In the early stages of his ministry, Calvin noticed that the city did not look or act as a reformed city.
    1. Calvin attempted to set up a number of reforms in the city.
    2. The city council did not favor these attempts.
- iii. On Easter Sunday in 1538, Calvin refused to give communion to the members of the city of Geneva.
    1. Calvin's action at the very least puts the city under church discipline, and at worst it excommunicates it.
    2. The city responded by voting Calvin out of his position and giving him forty-eight hours to vacate the city.
- iv. Calvin claimed in a letter to Heinrich Bullinger that the city of Geneva wanted preachers and not pastors.
    1. Up until the sixteenth century, the clergy had delivered the mass and performed the sacraments, but they had largely stayed out of the day-to-day life of the people.
    2. Calvin desired to perform a pastoral role amongst his flock, but they resisted.

D. Calvin's exile in Strasbourg
- i. Calvin traveled to Strasbourg from Geneva.
    1. While there, he married a widow, Idelette de Bure.
    2. He also wrote and published his first commentary on Scripture (on the book of Romans).
- ii. Meanwhile, Roman Catholic bishops and priests flooded Geneva in an attempt to regain it, and the people could not defend themselves against their teaching.
    1. The city pleaded with Calvin to return.
    2. Despite his temerity, Calvin returned to Geneva.

E. Calvin's return to Geneva (AD 1541)
- i. Calvin demanded that the city allow him to perform proper pastoral ministry.

1. The city, although not conducive in all matters, largely allowed Calvin to minister as he believed proper.
2. Calvin would serve at Geneva until the end of his life in 1564.

ii. Calvin served the Lord in a variety of ways during his pastorate at Geneva.

1. Calvin instituted and supported a large missionary movement.
   a. Between the 1540s and the 1550s, around two thousand Frenchman traveled to Geneva, studied, and were sent back into Roman Catholic France as underground missionaries.
   b. In the 1550s, the city of Geneva even sent missionaries to Brazil, where a church established by these missionaries still exists today.
2. Calvin accepted a number of refugees suffering for their reformed faith into the city of Geneva.
   a. An influx of citizens from Florence, a city where the Reformation never took root, settled in Geneva.
      1) Many of these refugees were skillful jewelers adept in making icons.
      2) Calvin recommended they use their skills to make watches instead.
   b. Marian refugees from England and Scotland settled in Geneva.
      1) These people fled from the Roman Catholic terror of Mary I ("Bloody Mary").
      2) The city of Geneva could not expand outward due to the large wall surrounding the city, so they expanded upwards on their houses to make room for the refugees.
      3) John Knox, the great Scottish Reformer, was great influenced by Calvin and Geneva.
3. Calvin contributed to the culture and the Reformed church in many, many ways, but he contributed particularly to the understanding of the believer's union with Christ.
   a. The doctrine of the union of Christ states that as the Spirit unites us to the Savior, we receive His righteousness and become joint-heirs to the kingdom of God.
   b. Calvin realized that this promise occurred *solus Christus*, in Christ alone.
   c. He knew that our salvation rested in Jesus, our sympathetic High Priest who suffered on our behalf and opened eternity to us through His love and grace.

STUDY QUESTIONS

1. The first book Calvin wrote was *Institutes of the Christian Religion*.
   a. True
   b. False

2. Calvin left France to study at Strasbourg under ___________.
   a. Heinrich Bullinger
   b. Ulrich Zwingli
   c. Martin Bucer
   d. Martin Luther

3. Calvin was persuaded to stay in Geneva and help establish the reformed church by ___________.
   a. Conrad Grebel
   b. John Knox
   c. Philip Melanchthon
   d. William Farel

4. Calvin instituted and supported a vibrant missions movement while serving in Geneva.
   a. True
   b. False

5. Calvin eventually returned to Paris, France, and established a church there that still exists today.
   a. True
   b. False

BIBLE STUDY AND DISCUSSION QUESTIONS

1. Did Calvin always pursue a career in ministry? How did the Lord convert Him? What is the *Institutes of the Christian Religion*? When did Calvin write it?

2. Who is William Farel? How did the people of Geneva receive Farel initially? How did Farel respond? How did he convince Calvin to stay in Geneva?

3. Why did the people of Geneva exile Calvin? Where did Calvin go, and what did he do while there?

4. Why did the people of Geneva request Calvin to return? How did Calvin respond?

5. Describe some of the reforms and movements Calvin instituted. What do his actions demonstrate? How are we united to Christ? How did Calvin's understanding of *solus Christus* affect his ministry?

6

Soli Deo Gloria: Glorifying God in Everything

MESSAGE INTRODUCTION

In 1 Corinthians 10:31, Paul says, "Whatever you do, do all to the glory of God." Do you find yourself divorcing your "religious life" from your "normal life"? Paul's exhortation makes this condition impossible, for every thought, word, and deed contributes to the Christian task of glorifying God. The Reformers of the sixteenth and seventeenth century knew this principle well, for they recovered it with much struggle from the Roman Catholic Church. *Soli Deo Gloria*, "the glory of God alone," drove them in every area of life, and they find this call a privilege bestowed on them by the grace of God through our precious Lord, Jesus.

SCRIPTURE READINGS

Psalm 68:19–20; 115:1; John 3:16; 1 Corinthians 10:23–11:1

TEACHING OBJECTIVES

1. To illustrate the place and importance of catechisms in the life of the church
2. To explain the historical circumstances leading to the formation of the Puritans
3. To relate the outcome of the Westminster Assembly and to demonstrate the centrality of *soli Deo gloria* in all that they did
4. To reinforce the need for all of God's people in all ages to proclaim the message of Christ crucified for the glory of God alone

QUOTATION

Question: What is your only comfort in life and death?
Answer: That I am not my own, but belong with body and soul both in life and in death to my faithful Savior Jesus Christ. He has fully paid for all my sins with His precious blood; He has set me free from all the power of the devil; He also preserves me in such

a way that without the will of my heavenly Father, not a hair can fall from my head; indeed, all things must work together for my salvation. Therefore, by His Holy Spirit, He also assures me of eternal life, and makes me heartily willing and ready from now on to live for Him.

—Question and Answer 1 from the *Heidelberg Catechism*

LECTURE OUTLINE

I. The Catechisms of the Reformation
  A. Martin Luther's *Children's Catechism*
    i. Luther believed that the Reformers must instruct the younger generation in the essential doctrines of Scripture.
      1. He charged his leaders in the community to write a catechism to teach children the basics of faith.
        a. Some were too moralistic.
        b. Others were too deep.
      2. Eventually, Luther decided to write the catechism himself.
    ii. Luther's catechism examined and taught the essential texts and creeds of Christianity to youth.
  B. The *Heidelberg Catechism*
    i. The *Heidelberg Catechism* consists of three sections: the misery of man, the redemption of man, and the gratitude due from man.
    ii. The first question and answer of the catechism delivers one of the most beautiful summaries of the gospel in all of theological literature.
  C. The *Westminster Shorter Catechism*
    i. In the 1640s, the Puritans developed a catechism for their children called the *Westminster Shorter Catechism.*
    ii. The first question and answer rivals the beauty of the first question and answer from the *Heidelberg Catechism.*
      1. The catechism asks, "What is the chief end of man."
      2. The answer: "Man's chief end is to glorify God and to enjoy Him forever."
      3. This answer refers to the Reformation principle of *soli Deo Gloria*: "the glory of God alone."

II. The Puritans
  A. The historical context for the emergence of the Puritans.
    i. Henry VIII made himself the supreme head of the Church of England by passing the Act of Supremacy in 1534.
      1. With this move, Henry separated the Church of England from the Roman Catholic Church.
      2. No theological overhaul existed in the church, but Henry passed this act to legitimize his annulment to Catherine of Aragon.

- ii. Under Edward the VI, Henry's son, and his advisor, Thomas Cranmer, the Reformation made great strides theologically.
- iii. When Edward died in 1553, Mary I ascended to the throne.
    1. Mary, a Roman Catholic labeled by Protestants as "Bloody Mary," persecuted those outside of the Roman Catholic Church.
    2. She set the Reformation in England back many years.
- iv. After Mary's death in 1558, her younger half-sister, Elizabeth I, took the throne and restored the Church of England (although she did relent from persecuting Roman Catholics severely).
    1. In 1558, Elizabeth passed the Act of Uniformity (a.k.a. "Conformity Laws"), which required religious practice to conform to the Church of England.
    2. A group of Protestants existed who, under good conscience, could not conform to this act. They were called non-conformists.
        - a. They were also called Separatists.
        - b. As a term of derision, they received the name "Puritans," because they were after a pure church.
- v. After James I succeeded Elizabeth I, he wrote the *Book of Sports* and required the Puritans to follow it.
    1. During his travel back to his homeland in Scotland, James would travel through Cambridge, a center of Puritan life and thought.
    2. While traveling through Cambridge on a Sunday, James noticed the children sitting around and not doing anything.
        - a. He inquired as to why this was occurring.
        - b. When he was told that the Puritans did not believe in the participation in physical sports on Sundays, he wrote the *Book of Sports* (which advocated recreation on Sunday) and required the Puritans to read and adhere to it.

B. The Westminster Assembly

- i. Under Charles I, James' successor, the Puritans experienced religious pressure.
    1. Charles I's desire to grasp more power and his inclination toward Roman Catholicism (intimated through his marriage as well as his appointment of church leaders such as William Laud), caused the Puritan faction in the British Parliament unease.
    2. Eventually, the Puritans in Parliament called for a restructuring of the Church of England in 1643 without Charles' assent.
    3. The assembly met at Westminster from 1643–1649 and produced the *Westminster Standards*, consisting of the *Westminster Confession of Faith*, the *Westminster Larger Catechism*, the *Westminster Shorter Catechism*, and the *Directory of Public Worship*.
        - a. The Scotch Presbyterians played an important role in assisting the Puritans.

b. These doctrines have become very much a part of the Reformed world.

ii. The tone of the *Westminster Standards* is set in the first question of the *Westminster Shorter Catechism.*

1. The catechism asks, "What is the chief end of man."
2. The answer: "Man's chief end is to glorify God and to enjoy Him forever."

a. Luther developed a word to capture the state of man: *incurvitas* ("turned in").

1) In our fallen state, human beings turn inwards for authority, fulfillment, and glory.

b. The Westminster Assembly understood this fallen state well, and they cut to the heart of the issue: man must live for the glory of God alone, *soli Deo Gloria.*

C. *Soli Deo Gloria*

i. The Reformers understood that the principle of *soli Deo Gloria* applied to all of life.

1. Luther and John Calvin understood that every vocation comes from God and should be performed to His glory.

a. Before the Reformation, only the clergy possessed vocations (derived from the Latin word for "calling").

b. Luther and Calvin applied this word to all people and claimed that each served a sentinel post for God.

1) A sentinel was an elite guard.
2) All men have the privilege of serving the Lord in this important position.

ii. This study has demonstrated through the life of the Reformers the importance of proclaiming Christ crucified for the glory of God, and the call to preach this message applies today just as forcefully as it applied to Luther, Calvin, and the other Reformers of the sixteenth and seventeenth centuries.

STUDY QUESTIONS

1. Martin Luther wrote the ____________.
   a. *Westminster Shorter Catechism*
   b. *Heidelberg Catechism*
   c. *Belgic Confession*
   d. *Children's Catechism*

2. Under Edward VI and Thomas Cranmer, the Reformation of the Church of England suffered greatly.
   a. True
   b. False

3. The group who resisted the Act of Uniformity (a.k.a. the "Conformity Laws") were known as the ___________.
   a. Puritans
   b. Separatists
   c. Non-conformists
   d. All of the above

4. Charles I called for the Westminster Assembly to reform the Church of England.
   a. True
   b. False

5. *Incurvitas* means ___________.
   a. "turned in"
   b. "turned out"
   c. "inside out"
   d. "incumbent"

BIBLE STUDY AND DISCUSSION QUESTIONS

1. Why did Luther see a need for a catechism? What three catechisms did Dr. Nichols describe in this lecture? What is the first question and answer to the *Westminster Shorter Catechism*?

2. How and why did the Puritans come into existence?

3. Why did the Puritans in Parliament call for a restructuring of the Church of England? Did Charles I agree? What did the Westminster Assembly produce?

4. How did the principle of *soli Deo Gloria* influence the Westminster Assembly?

5. How does the principle of *soli Deo Gloria* apply to all of life? How did the Reformers, such as Luther and Calvin, view it? Take some time to meditate on the Reformers Dr. Nichols has covered in this series. How should their doctrine and example influence you today?